THE TRUTH ABOUT THE FACTS

THE TRUTH ABOUT THE FACTS

Change Your Thinking, Change Your Life

DR. LEVEN "CHUCK" WILSON

WINSTON SALEM

THE TRUTH ABOUT THE FACTS: CHANGE YOUR THINKING, CHANGE YOUR LIFE

Soft cover ISBN: 978-0-9988313-4-3
E-Book ISBN: 978-0-9988313-5-0

Library of Congress Cataloging-in-Publication Data
Names: Wilson, Leven
Title: The truth about the facts/Leven Wilson;
LCCN: 2017959961
LC record available at https://lccn.loc.gov/2017959961

Cooke House Publishing
(a division of Cooke Consulting & Creations, LLC)
Winston-Salem, NC
publishing@cookecc.org

This book and all Cooke House Publishing books are available at bookstores and distributors worldwide.

Printed in the United States of America.- First Edition

Praise for Chuck Leven and *The Truth About the Facts*

Dr. Leven "Chuck" Wilson is a spiritually gifted change agent. He uses his talent to encourage and empower people to move beyond their personal and professional limitations. I raised him and I'm super proud of this guy. Purchase a few copies of *The Truth About the Facts* and experience the "Chuckster" for yourself. Friends, let's support this young Christian mogul!

—John P. Kee
National Recording Artist
Pastor, New Life City of Praise

Chuck has always been a gifted storyteller. I was thrilled to see his stories and observations in written form so that more people could learn from his experiences and analysis. We all need healing in our lives, now, more than ever. This was a great reminder of where I need to focus some of my energy personally and professionally.

—Jessica R. Garlock, MSW, LSW
Hawaii Pacific University

My personal journey to finding and effectively dealing with the truths and facts in my life has been deeply enhanced by having access to Dr. Chuck Wilson. When I met him in 2016, I needed a mindset change that would help me better navigate my future. He challenged me upon our first meeting and he continues to challenge me now. I am grateful for his wisdom and very thankful that, through this book, his words will help others to think beyond their personal limits.

—Holly Wilson, MA

The fact is that each day working with Chuck is a real-life master class. I end each day with several takeaways that not only enrich my life, but the lives of those I come in contact with. He has taught me that at any age you can pursue your dreams, the importance of having crucial conversations, and to always look for the best in others. It doesn't matter how many degrees you have, every member of the team is a valuable asset. My truth is that gratefulness flows from my heart when I think about how God has used this man to bless me and my family. Chuck, may God continue to bless you to be a blessing to others. Much love.

—Robin Wise

This thought-provoking and spiritual awakening guide to the future is a must read for all who are searching for truth, peace, and fulfillment.

—Delisa Sauders, Ph.D.

CONTENTS

FOREWORD

ONE MAY WONDER, when does he sleep as he may be in three different cities in one day, or how does he find the time to prepare for the innumerable speaking engagements. If asked to encourage a particular underserved population, even with a full docket, he is there. Most encouraging moments remembered are those privileged chats engaged in extemporaneous conversations. You walk away wanting more, because the experience leaves you feeling different; somewhat changed. This book will transform your life. I consider Dr. Leven "Chuck" Wilson a spiritually gifted person. As a change agent, he uses his talent and personal experiences to show others how to move the needles and mountains that impede their progress. As a social worker, he is positioned to look beyond the surface of conversations and break down barriers so that people can freely pursue worthy goals. He is the guy who made the single mother feel empowered to apply to law school, or the wayward teen apply and get accepted to a prestigious university. Chuck has helped so many others who have gone on to develop healthier habits like the young lady with noticeable increased self-confidence, self-worth, and self-esteem just from their encounters.

The Truth About the Facts is an enthusiastic celebration of living one's life to the fullest potential. This book presents a new lens from which to view past and current circumstances. Through the art of storytelling, Chuck encourages you to disrupt the status quo, have courageous conversations, and to boldly tell the truth. It is a unique tribute to selflessness, perseverance, tenacity, and a deep desire to be *stupidly* happy. There are several vignettes that intertwine and carry the theme of truthfulness, in a very engaging way. Readers will gain a broader perspective of self and the importance of communicating the truth. These stories are thought provoking, spiritual-awakening moments, and jaw-dropping events. It is captivating. A must read, if you want to be set free.

—Yvonne Kelly Montell, Ed.D.
aka "Dr. Yo"

PREFACE

I WAS INSPIRED to write this book mainly to encourage people to face the truths and facts of their lives. However, I wanted to understand my own truths and facts as it has afforded me some positive processes and outcomes, and some that were not. I was convicted by a sermon entitled *Faith in the Face of the Facts* by Joel Gregory. In order to understand faith, you must know the facts. Furthermore, in order to understand the facts, you've got to know the truth.

As a social worker for many years, I've heard countless stories and experienced unforgettable moments. *The Truth About the Facts* was written to assist individuals, families, and communities to change. It is about healing, better introspective assessment, and finding the ability to be a free spirit.

I want to recognize and dedicate this book to my mother, Dr. Brenda Rowdy. She raised three kids with integrity, love, and 'other people' thinking. She is my mother and my father. To my readers, I challenge you to know the truth about the facts in your life. This book is designed to help you reset and respect your future, which will ultimately become your history.

—Dr. Leven "Chuck" Wilson, II

CHAPTER 1

WHAT IS TRUTH?

"At the core of truth is healing, even though there may be a battle in the process."

THE TRUTH IS IN THE WHY

WHEN WE TALK about what the truth is, we need to first recognize that the truth is tough. There is just no way to get around that. Truth can be damaging, it can be peaceful, and it can be harmful. It can be a variety of things, but what I want you to understand is that truth is the ultimate healer. A lot of times we just want to get to what is. I'm sure you've heard the statement, "It is what it is." Well, it IS what it is. That is just a fact. The focus of this book is to analyze the process and everything that led to that fact. The truth is in the process.

I'll give you an example. If you say that you hate your dad, that may be a fact, but what is the truth about that? What caused that? What caused you to think like that? What emotions, feelings, and thoughts drove you to that? Was that something that was transferred to you by your mother, aunts and uncles, or friends? Have they been influential in forming your perception about your dad? Have you communicated with your dad? Have you given him the opportunity to state his facts?

Getting down to the nooks and crannies of why something is good or bad—I mean really pouring down into something, really chewing the fat on what put us here—those are the truths. How did this become a feeling or thought in the first place? What you do with those facts and truths determine *how* those truths create life or death situations, problems, and concerns. I believe that truths and how you perceive truths can cause you to grow or remain stagnant, because if you perceive the truth as one thing and it really isn't the truth, then you must examine why you look at it that way. Are you basing your truth on your feelings, thoughts, and experiences? Are you basing your truth on the dynamics of past, current, and possibly even future situations? Look at the way that you treat your family, your friends, and your significant other. Why do you treat them the way that you do? *That's* where the truth is. The truth is in the why.

When you are asking yourself why, you're beginning the process of truth-finding. Be willing to accept and embrace the truth, whether good or bad. You can only grow from truth. One thing that is very important to understand is that we all lie. A person who says they don't lie is, in fact, a liar.

We lie about what we often consider very little things. For example, someone you know says to you, "Let's go out to eat." You choose a particular restaurant because you think it's the one they want to go to. Now, you really don't want to go there. You *really* don't even want to go out to eat. You're just responding to the question and responding to their feelings. That can be a good thing to respond to their feelings, probably considering the things that they've done for you in the past. But since you don't even want to go to dinner, even in making those considerations, it is still a lie.

The challenge in every area of your life is to look for truth. It must be a lifelong journey, a minute-to-minute process. You must also be forgiving of other people. A lot of times, you don't know what the road to truth is for most people. Sometimes you'll hold people hostage to your expectations of them because you think that they are not truthful or didn't tell the truth about one thing or another. They may not have known what their *why* was. They may not have known how they got into that situation. They may be numb. I'm sure you've heard people say that they are numb. When you are numb, that means you are tuned out, disconnected, and refuse to see the relativity of something. When you are in that space, how can you find truth? How can you expect others to find truth? How can you find truth if you aren't looking for it? Work to be more in tune with looking for truth, not for the "gotcha" or surprise moment, but for the living moment. When you operate from that mindset, you will discover yourself to be much more willing to offer grace, internally and externally.

This book is about healing. It is about resolution, life, and ultimately being at peace. This book is also about restoration and hope, and I know the commonality is truth. Now, I do want to caution you not to place truth in jail by setting it within rigid parameters and surrounding it with attacks, hatred, bigotry, sabotage, or anything negative. When you do that, you will find yourself right back at the beginning of the process. As I have stated, looking for truth is a lifelong journey, but do yourself a favor and honor the truth as you find it. Learn the truth, embrace the truth, and grow from the truth.

THE TRUTH IS IN RESPECT

Okay, now that you understand the importance of examining the truth, this is your opportunity to take it to another level. What are you going to do with the truth? Now that you have walked down that road of truth, where are you going to place it? Are you going to communicate and share it? There is respect for self and others in the process of truth-finding. Communicate your truth so that others may benefit from it.

My mama, Dr. Brenda Rowdy, was a tough woman when she was raising me. Though she was a short woman, she was tough as nails! I used to wonder why my mama was so tough on me. Now don't get me wrong, she wasn't tough on me in a bad way. She was a very loving mama to me as a child and young person. To this day, I can say that I have, unequivocally, the best mama in the world, but growing up I couldn't understand her personality. I didn't know who she really was because I did not know the truths about her life. One fact is that she is my mama. Another fact is that she is the greatest mama in the world. An additional fact is that she was tough as hell. Those are all facts to me. How she got that way is what the truth is.

When Mama was working on her doctorate, she had to write her autobiography. I had the chance to read it in my late thirties. I discovered that my mama had been through so many things as a child. From being inappropriately touched as a young lady, to witnessing her mother beaten to death in front of her by her boyfriend, my mama experienced things that are difficult for me to imagine. She did not have a relationship with her dad who was not in her life. She also grew up during a time when she saw a lot of injustices, unfair treatment of women and people of color, and unfair treatment based on class. She taught me to be an advocate, but I didn't know why. All I knew is that she was always fighting for something. The truth of the matter is that her experiences were daunting, troubling, catastrophic, and damaging, but they were also rewarding, healing, and restorative. They led her to be a great mother.

The truth of the matter is that her experiences were daunting, troubling, catastrophic, and damaging, but they were also rewarding, healing, and restorative.

I have found that most of the time truth, no matter how bad it is, will lead you to your destiny. You must, however, embrace the truth and communicate it because people don't know your truth unless you articulate it. How you got there is the root, and there is power in communicating that journey.

After reading my mother's autobiography, I learned so many things about the facts of her life, but more importantly, I learned to respect my mother in a new way. I'd always respected her as my mama because she demanded that respect and she deserved it. The gift of her communicating her life story and allowing me access to it, is what allowed me to respect her as a woman. That is the part that gave me peace, joy, and those intangible things that I was never able to grasp or articulate as a child and young adult. The truth of *her* life story helped to create *my* character. Once I learned my mother's reasons why and got a better understanding of her truth, I was better equipped to understand some of my own reasons why. This is a large part of my fortitude to fight for various causes to this day.

THE TRUTH IS IN HEALING

Finding my own truth started from trying to figure out why I never received a card from my father for my birthday. It started when I wanted to know why I had feelings of wanting a certain image growing up and why I wanted to look a certain way. I mean, everyone who knows me knows that I am one of the best dressers in the world, but why? I was a big guy, but nobody in my family was big, so I wanted to know why. I didn't really eat that much, but I was just a big person.

During that time in my life, I would use clothes to camouflage how I really felt. I would use clothes to mask my insecurities. I used clothes to present an image of an extrovert. It may even be surprising to people who have seen me out in the community engaging with the public and fighting against injustices in the world, to know that I am actually a shy person. I like being by myself, but my gifts afford me the opportunity to be around people all the time. But the real Chuck? I am cool with being by myself.

When I look over my life and all my accomplishments, I ask myself why did I accomplish these things? Why did I do it at a certain time? I'm a late bloomer in certain areas. Why did I even think about doing certain things? Why don't I have kids or a dog? See, I always try to figure out why.

I had a great childhood! I took drum and bass lessons, and even traveled the world because my mom worked for an airline. I sang in a professional choir. However, I saw a lot of things that didn't match. The actions of some didn't seem to match what they sung about. I didn't want to be that kind of person that I could not respect. I still don't want to be that kind of person. So, I thought since I couldn't find the reasons why externally, I had to find them within. I had to start with myself. I had to come to terms with the fact that my father was never going to tell the truth about his lack of relationship with me, and it has always been too painful for my mother to discuss with me.

My mother did share with me a very painful truth about my dad. She told me that my dad beat her up to abort me. So, knowing the truth of his abuse, and knowing that my own dad tried to abort me by kicking my mama in her stomach, makes it extremely difficult to receive his sentiments as truth when I hear my dad say how much he loves me and is proud of me when I visit him. I wanted to know what that kick meant. Now, because I would never get the truth about what that kick meant from him, I decided to dig down into myself to find out what the kick caused. Did it cause me to be an overachiever? Did it cause me to have so many emotions as a child that it is difficult for me to even articulate today, in my fifties?

So, that's why I must deal with the truth. If I don't, I cannot really get to who I am. Because I have gone through that process, I know that introducing myself to myself is better than money or having walls full of awards (and I have more than I can count). But, how is that going to help someone else? That is the question. It may have started with the kick. That kick put something in me. I wasn't even aware when it happened, and it may have been designed to kill me, but it gave me something very powerful.

Pursuing truth is why I ask so many questions. I am constantly looking at people and stuff around me, just trying to figure out things, but I've also tried to figure out my own why. Sometimes the truth is not in you. It's somewhere else. When that is the case, you must investigate yourself, and I think a lot of times, when you look at the things that you do that are wrong, you should ask yourself why you do those things. Where did they come from? I didn't process things the same way that most kids did in school. It was like I was standing outside of myself looking at me. I became more aware of my disposition and appearance, but why? Was I hiding pain? I didn't understand why my mama had me in Cub Scouts and Boy Scouts. My mama made sure that I was around great men, but it didn't take away the existence of pain that not having my father in my life caused me. At the core of truth is healing, even though there may be a battle in the process. You know, you must find your dirt to grow, and I look for my dirt. I investigate my own dirt. To push through the dirt and see the truth, that is where healing and success live.

THE TRUTH IS IN THE DIRT

Most people don't want to face truths because of the battle. Some people like the fight. Some create them, but it is important to get past the battle, the war, the conflict. We are born in struggle. We are human. Hell, we are made of dirt and clay, so there has to be some trouble somewhere. Think about it, all precious commodities have dirt, sand, and "stuff" associated with them. You cannot find gold or anything good on this earth without going through the dirt.

Truth is never on the surface! It's always under the dirt. So, GO THROUGH THE DIRT! Your destiny, resolutions, and even your ability to move forward is going to be there when you push through the dirt. To get through the dirt, sometimes you may need an ax or maybe even a bomb. For more delicate work, you may need a chisel. When you are processing and looking for truth, you must ask yourself what kinds of tools do you need. Do you need a listening tool or an action tool? Do you need a communication tool or do you need the tool of silence? It may be an outright fight! It might be a brass knuckle, down and dirty fight to dig through to the truth! Don't brawl to kill. Brawl to get the truth! If we look at truth from that perspective, we will feel better. We will know how to treat each other.

THE TRUTH IS IN HONOR

Let me talk to the men for a moment. It is said that men are creatures of sensation. My mother taught me that I am responsible for the responses that I want. And I am not talking about men in a relationship. I am not even talking about men trying to woo a woman. I'm just talking about how we treat all women. We have an obligation to restore, respect, and honor all women, regardless of looks, hairstyles, or nails. Whether they are naturalists or implant experts, it doesn't matter. When we show women respect and honor, and not just show them our asses when we don't get our way, that means we are moving closer to dealing with the truth of who we are.

I heard a story once of a man who entered a restaurant and saw a very beautiful woman. She was the only other patron in the restaurant, but had there been a crowd, her beauty would have pushed through the sea of faces. To him, she was the most beautiful woman he had ever seen. He approached her and told her of her beauty and shared that he thought that he was in love with her and wanted to marry her immediately. She asked how he could know that he loved her when he had just met her. He told her that it did not matter because he was very sure because she was the most beautiful woman in the world and he wanted to spend the rest of his life with her.

She responded that before he could make that decision, he must first meet her sister and her cousin. The man agreed because the woman told him that her sister and cousin were the most beautiful women in the world, in her mind. While waiting for the woman's sister and her cousin, the man could not take his eyes off this beautiful woman. When the cousin and sister walked in, the man looked hard at both women. He even took his glasses off to make sure that his eyes were not playing tricks on him. The man was troubled as to why this beautiful woman would say that her sister and cousin were the most beautiful women in the world, because they certainly were not. They didn't even compare to her, from a physical perspective.

If you really know what the truth is, you don't have to go looking for something better!

The man looked at this beautiful woman and shared his disappointment at her suggestion that he see her sister and cousin before committing to her. The beautiful woman asked him, "How could you tell me you love me and want to be with me for the rest of your life, and look for something else?" The truth of the matter is that he didn't know what he was looking for. He didn't understand his own process. If you really know what the truth is, you don't have to go looking for something better! Truth *can* be absolute in that context.

I have to talk to the women, too. Don't make a man lie because you aren't being truthful or don't want to know the truth. Don't say, "I got somethin' for ya, Sugah," when you know you don't! Don't promise hope and deliver chaos. Don't promise passion and total accessibility when you have absolutely no intention of fulfilling either of those promises. Understand that when you refuse to even respond to his touch or refuse his kind gestures believing that because you got his attention with those promises, that you can keep his attention with words that keep him hanging on. The *truth* of the matter is that the man will not wait forever. If you don't understand the truth behind why you made those promises in the first place, you will have a very difficult time figuring out your own truth, especially in the context of a relationship with a man. You must honor yourself in the process of finding the truth and exploring personal and interpersonal relationships.

Now, you know that children are not off the hook here. Children, make it a point to be givers and not takers. In fact, be givers without expectation of reciprocation. Aspire to be altruistic in all your pursuits. Parents, it is your responsibility to teach your children these values. We know that children will always want the newest phone and the hottest clothes, but what will this mean to them when they begin to examine the truth about who they are? You will create little monsters if you give them everything without teaching them the value of money and the value in themselves and others. You may be shaping their intellect, but are you shaping their character? Stuff won't buy truth. Stuff just looks for stuff.

Truth may or may not be absolute. Truth is pure in thought, agenda, and process. You must really deal with all aspects of the truth and when you don't, that is where problems arise. It is vital to use truth to honor and not destroy. Use truth to respect. Use truth to discover and build even when the situation is bad. Even after war, one of the first things that governments do is put money together to help restore the country that has been destroyed.

Don't allow people, places, or things to impact your truths or facts! Don't let people get you off your truth! Don't settle for the relationship because of the money or the sex or overall stability. Don't sabotage yourself by being around people because you think they can take you places! Don't settle for the appearance, but engage with the truth. The truth will be your vehicle. But when you settle for ass, abs, and tits looking for satisfaction, you never get to the truth. The truth may be in someone who you would not have chosen. The truth can be catastrophic and the facts detrimental. Now, there is nothing wrong with working toward ass, abs and tits, but that is not the final product of what you want the truth to be. Don't look for truth with a superficial lens.

HOMEWORK? YES, YOU HAVE HOMEWORK.

So, with all of this in mind, I have homework for you. When you wake up every morning and do your daily devotion, meditation, yoga, or whatever it is that you do to get your day started, make it your mission to discover truth within yourself. Look for the plank in your eye and the thorn in your flesh. Look at yourself in your rawest form and ask "why." You know that this will not be easy, but I already told you that you must dig through the dirt to get to your truth. It's time to start digging! I don't want you to do this to beat yourself up, but to heal yourself, to grow, to be who you are supposed to be, to help someone else, to strengthen your ability to think about other people (other-people thinking), to honor someone else, and not just relish on the good and bad parts of you.

Sometimes you may only see the good in yourself and demonstrate some narcissistic tendencies and behaviors. However, when you do see the good in yourself, be thankful for the goodness, but ask yourself why you have it. What is your purpose for having a good heart? What is the purpose of you giving and sharing? When you are looking for the truth in yourself, don't just look for the dark stuff. Look at yourself in totality. There is goodness in all people. There is something great about everybody alive. There are also some things that need to be fixed and changed about everybody alive, too. That is where you find the truth. Let's commit to the work of finding the truth.

CHAPTER 2

WHAT ARE FACTS?

"Finding facts becomes a mission of discovery."

WE CAN LOOK at facts from many different perspectives. We can look at it from a scientific perspective, religious perspective, or even a sociological perspective. A *fact* is basically something that exists, something that is there. You have two legs. That is a fact. You can see your legs and can touch them. Another fact is that you have a car that you can physically get into and drive. A fact is that you have a home where you can unlock the door, come and go as you please, prepare meals, and rest.

Some facts that we struggle with are those facts that we cannot touch. We cannot really see a headache. You can tell me that you have a headache, but how do I know that you have one. You cannot see or touch a headache, you can only feel a headache. In the context of this book, I am talking about the facts that we can and cannot see. In Chapter One, I talked about truths. For me, truth is about processes, events, actions, and activities that lead to facts. Facts are more of what actually is.

When we talk about facts, we can talk about intangible things such as hurt, joy, pain, discouragement, and encouragement. But what do facts mean? In this book, it is important to determine and understand what the facts are, whether tangible or intangible. If it is tangible, facts are easier to deal with because you know that if you can put your hands on it, break or build it, paint it or burn it, lift it, change it, or float it, then it gives you a different way to look at things.

When you cannot see it or put your hands on it, that is where the problem arises. Sometimes our facts become distorted because there are so many competing interests. For example, love does not have legs, feet, and arms in the tangible sense, but you should be able to use your senses to demonstrate love, which helps you determine whether it is a fact or not. When we go through life dealing with situations, we must examine how we deal with them. How do we know if someone loves us or if they do not love us? Now, we must start to examine the process and ask where the feet, legs, and eyes are. When you say you love someone, you must have a plan for that relationship. It is a little like making a major purchase, where you have done your research and investigated your desires and commitment to making that purchase. You must go into a relationship with a plan to sustain the relationship and you must make a real commitment to your plan to manage and sustain that love. The intangible means that you must go on a fact-finding mission to determine the facts. It becomes a mission of discovery. It is an ongoing mission. Facts can change, move, remain stagnant, or grow.

I think it broadens our view of facts. Now, we do not want to spin it to make it a fact, but looking at the evidence of the facts is vitally important. That is why we must understand the truths. Truths + Truths = Facts. There must be a formula. It is like an algebraic formula, where A multiplied by B plus C may equal a fact. It can be quite complex. The issue is when we want to add things that are not true to the formula, then the facts become alternative, and we would want to stay away from that. That is why it is also important to communicate and understand how you discover facts, because in communication you may feel things one way based on the way something is said, but it may not have been delivered in the way that you could best receive it.

When we look at that formula of discovering the process of finding the truth and do not understand the major premises regarding what is after the equal sign, then our truths are always cloudy. That is why we feel unresolved and unhappy because our formula is incorrect. Conversely, we can feel resolved and happy when our formula is correct. The most important thing in this chapter is understanding your formula to the facts. Your mission to discover the facts should not be done alone. The mission should be done with people, places, and things that you have found the truth in. You must confide in people that will tell you that yes means yes and no means no and will not sugarcoat your messes, because that is the only way that we going to get to truth.

The formula must be truth + truth. Actually, it really does not matter which symbol you use. The symbol determines the outcome, but the integers must be truth. That is why communication is important. If we look at the climate of our country, our facts are distorted because we do not know the truth. We do not know our history on all sides. If the formula is not truth + truth, we will not get to the facts. Your truth can have some information that my truth does not have, but you must have some evidence that your truth is actually the truth. Whether you are talking about world economy, politics, or are around the kitchen table with your family, we must be willing to listen and evaluate without the intent to do wrong because we do not want the truth. A lot of times people will want to do harm to you or place fear in you because they do not want the truth. This does not always have to be external. It can be an internal process as well.

In the first chapter, we talked about how some people use clothes, food, and other distractions to not deal with the truth. When you are dealing with yourself, you cannot get to a fact if you are not willing to have a courageous conversation with yourself. In the truth formula, it must begin with you telling the absolute truth to yourself. If you cannot tell the truth to yourself, you cannot tell the truth to anyone else. You only get fragmented pieces of the truth. If you start the process, at least you are making the effort to move forward, but it is hard to say to someone, "Just tell the truth," when you are dealing with pain, history, dynamics, and different competing interests.

There is a process to telling the truth and that is why it is so important to have a formula. Sometimes that formula may need to be tweaked. You may have to add some components of truth to it. If two sisters are having a debate over something that happened between their parents and both sisters have valid points and evidence to back up their points, but they are still at an impasse, the sisters may have to go and get their grandmother to tell her version based on her own perspective. She may have heard it a different way, and the addition of her view may end the debate between the sisters.

Facts cannot live in isolation. They cannot live in a silo. Facts are meant to live like an octopus with many tentacles, changing, moving and growing things, and giving things life. Your facts are not truly facts if you cannot face them. You cannot fix anything that you cannot face, but there is a process to it and that is the formula. Remember that Truths + Truths = Facts. You must face your truths, no matter the level of difficulty, in order to get to your facts.

CHAPTER 3

CONSUMED BY WHAT YOU CANNOT CONTROL

"When you are trapped between truths and facts, it can be a life sentence with no visible opportunity for parole."

ARE YOU CONSUMED by something that you can't control? Are you currently in a place of living or being that is not working toward your best interests, but you cannot seem to make sense of how to control it? Are you existing in a relationship or doing something that you either must do or feel like you must do to survive?

I am going to share a story with you. I am a social worker by trade and I currently work with over two hundred clients. While each client is unique, I find that many times there is a thread that seems to connect most, if not all of them. Each client is trying to progress in life, trying to discover the facts and the truths of who they are. They come to me because they are stuck and are seeking assistance with moving the needle toward who they actually want to be. Each client progresses at his or her own pace, and some are so trapped that they believe there is no end in sight to the perils of their situation. I would like to offer a small portion of one client's story to help you get to a better understanding of your own facts and truths. For the purposes of confidentiality, no identifying information will be used.

I have been working with one particular gentleman for some time now. He is a tall and handsome gentleman. A professional with an honorable career. He is a Southern, Christian man. Many years ago, he met a beautiful Southern, Christian woman. She was very attractive and was also a young professional. When he met her, it may not have been love at first sight, but it was something that he had not experienced with any other woman during his life.

As a young Christian couple, the two dated and honored the Christian values with which they were raised. During their courtship, they communicated well and had fun together. They enjoyed each other's company and wanted to be around each other as much as possible. Though it was difficult for him on a physical level, the young man respected his girlfriend enough to agree when she shared that she did not want to engage in premarital sex. After dating for a while, they both realized that they loved each other deeply and decided to seal their union before God in holy matrimony. As they embarked on this new journey together, it seemed to the young man that this was a fairytale that would surely involve a happily ever after.

On the night of the honeymoon, the new husband was excited about making love to his wife after a few years of dating. He felt as though he was bursting at the seams, ready to share the physical manifestation of his love. He imagined that she shared the same excitement, and he worked to make it the night of her dreams. In a room filled with roses and beautiful music playing, he began to romance his wife. As they continued to enjoy each other, his wife shared that she was on her menstrual cycle and did not feel comfortable consummating their marriage that night. Although he was disappointed, he was still elated that they would be able to consummate their marriage in a few days. He had waited this long, and he knew that a few more days would not matter very much to him.

After the honeymoon was over, the couple was at home getting settled into their new lives together. Still excited at the prospect of consummating their marriage, the young husband set the stage again to make love to his wife. As he looked at this beautiful woman, who he viewed as the ultimate manifestation of God's creation, she looked him in the eyes and told him that she was not ready. She needed more time. He was amazed by her declaration, but remained patient because he knew that she was a virgin. Well, at least that was the assumption because they never actually talked about it. He assumed she was and he knew he was not. He could not imagine that someone that beautiful could be a virgin.

He remained patient and weeks turned into months, and months turned into two years. The couple engaged in some foreplay and heavy petting, but he found himself in a constant state of shock because he always had to go to a secret place to take care of his physical needs, while confused about what led their marriage to this place. This secrecy is intricately connected with their image. On the surface, the couple was beautiful, and everyone assumed their marriage was filled with passion. They had a beautiful home in an exclusive neighborhood. They drove luxury cars, and each were making their mark in their respective professional fields. Underneath the surface, however, there was no passion, only a husband that felt demeaned and humiliated by his wife's rejection.

He found himself dealing with a lot of competing interests. What about having children? Would that ever be a possibility? When he broached the subject with his wife, she responded with inconsolable crying. Still, he remained patient with her and asked her to join him in couples therapy. During the first session, the therapist asked, "What is the problem with consummating your relationship?" The room fell silent and the wife began to cry. She left the session and never returned. The husband stayed and expressed his feelings and thoughts about being patient for the two years of their marriage, but found no resolution during the session.

Two years turned to three years, three years turned to four, and four years turned to five. By now you are probably wondering what in the world would cause this man to stay with his wife after five years of never having sexual contact. Now, I need you to understand that this man is a tall, relatively charming fellow, who never subscribed to the alternative option of going outside of the marriage to meet his physical needs. Sometime ago, he met a woman at his place of business. Though she did not speak English well, her eyes spoke to him. He and this woman developed a great friendship. In a way, he grew to love her. Even though they did not have a sexual relationship, she provided the emotional connection that he had been waiting for from his wife. When she cooked food at home, she brought food to him at work. She treated him better than he was treated at home. Because he was still married, he did not know how to engage this woman. He loved the affection he received from her, but he did not feel worthy of that treatment.

Instead, he ruminated on why his wife did not desire him. He began to work out to make himself more attractive to her. He began to make excuses for her refusal of him. Maybe she was molested as a child. Maybe she had a physical issue that was too embarrassing for her to face within or share with him. Maybe she had a phobia about sex. Maybe she only agreed to marry him out of pity for him. Whatever it was, he was unwilling to throw her under the bus. In short, he internalized the rejection. This impacted his ability to excel in his profession. He maintained his career, but never reached his full potential because he was constantly consumed with why his wife agreed to marriage but not to sexual contact with him. As time continued, the small amount of foreplay and heavy petting that he experienced with her before became less and less. It was like they became roommates and he took it upon himself to adopt a martyr mentality, truly believing that he could fix whatever was going on with her.

She later told him one August day that she never wanted to have children, and this only served to compound his pain and feelings of rejection. He was now left to wonder why he made the choices that he made regarding his faithfulness. He also wondered why he never imagined that she did not want children with him. Despite him feeling deceived by his wife, she appeared oblivious to the things that he is enduring because of this loveless marriage. He stopped checking in with her to see if her decision changed. He was distraught by her declaration about not wanting children, and of course, he blamed himself. Was this because he did not have a father growing up? Was he not expressing himself fully as a husband in his wife's eyes? Were his expectations of a loving and sex-filled marriage too high, because he never actually had an example of a healthy marriage growing up? Could his wife be afraid that their child would be broken like him? He already carried the weight of being the first male in his family to complete college, have a professional career, and get married. He wanted to break the cycle of his family history by being perfect. In his pursuit of perfection for everyone else, he lost himself.

By the time he arrived at my office five years ago, after many years of counseling, he was already in tears. He confided that he shed tears every day in private. He was consumed by what he thought he could not control. Though he maintains a certain facade for the public view, he is a very sad and reclusive gentleman in private. He has now been married to the same woman, in a marriage that has never been consummated, for 15 years. He has dedicated his love, energy, and emotions to a woman who has not reciprocated.

The first five minutes of each of our sessions involves him breaking into tears, due to the comfort he feels in being able to talk freely and openly about this situation with another male. He learned very early that this was not something that he could share with his friends and family. He was afraid that they would view him as stupid or a loser. Being able to share his feelings with another male in a nonjudgmental space has been cathartic in some ways, but he is still far from being able to fully deal with the truths and facts of his marriage.

The situation is believable because I know it to be an actual situation, yet on so many levels, it is unbelievable. He has maintained his decision not to cheat on his wife, and mostly feels that if he divorces her, no one will ever truly want to be with him. He is also afraid of being able to tell the truth about why he is having an affair or seeking divorce, when everything looks so perfect from the outside. The truth to date is that there is sadness and dishonesty, in the form of no communication, between the couple. He does not hate his wife, but he has never been loved by her as his wife, so he does not feel that connection. It is more like a sibling relationship.

Work is all that he must cling to these days. He does not feel safe sharing any of this information with his family for fear of being judged and facing more rejection from the only people that show him love. They have already noticed that he looks sad most of the time, that he is not as sociable as he was years ago, and that he no longer seems interested in maintaining a high level of style. He knows that they know, but he simply cannot bring himself to divulge the truth and talk about the facts of his marriage to them. He could receive assistance from them, but he refuses to let them in on a deeper level. He has even sought guidance from God, but still has no answers to this problem. He remains consumed by something that he feels he cannot control. Years ago, he made the decision to love, honor, and respect his wife, but the outcomes are not what he expected.

In the above story, it is important to look at the integers and symbols. As we begin to work things through and talk, I would offer that right now he is at a negative sum. An easy example is: -10+(10)=0. Either the integers or the symbols must change. Those are the truths about the facts. If he truly desires to move beyond anxious days and sleepless nights, he must change the integers or the symbols. What does that mean? Well, he must make some hard decisions.

He must deal with the facts of his marriage and tell the truth to himself and possibly others. What he has been doing for 15 years is not working because of his refusal to deal with the truths about the facts. He has been trapped in between truths and facts, and his hope is that he will get to the age where he no longer desires sexual contact with his wife. If he desires to remain stagnant, then he does not need to change his formula at all, but on some level, he needs to analyze why this is working for him. What is he gaining from his misery? Why does he want to live the rest of his life in this way? The facts are the facts and the truth is the truth, and either way, he must decide about the integers and symbols of his life.

This story is for anyone who feels like you are consumed by what you cannot control. You must start with a confession. You must tell someone who will hold your secrets to his or her heart. Because this gentleman is chained by the past, present and apparently, the future, he cannot make a change because of the fear that it would destroy his family and hers. It would destroy the semblance of love that everyone else thought was there. It would be destructive because no one knows the truth, but him and his wife.

The foundation of any relationship must be based on truth, not just the fact that you love, care, and want to spend the rest of your life with someone. Before you say, "I do," you must understand the truths about why you love them and why they love you, as well as how you love them in word and actions and how they reciprocate that love. You must view this from all perspectives and define the meaning of that love. How would you define it from physical, emotional, financial, mental and educational perspectives? From every part of your existence, how will you define love? How will you define care from each of those perspectives? Marriage is not always easy, so you need to define how you will care for your spouse during those darker times and how your spouse will care for you. How will you define each new day? How will you navigate your journey together?

The foundation of any relationship must be based on truth, not just the fact that you love, care, and want to spend the rest of your life with someone.

This young man had facts about the state of his marriage but no truths because he did not know his wife's reasons for her behavior, and now the facts have taken on a new definition. He remains consumed by what he cannot control.

This book is designed to help you not be consumed by things that you believe are out of your control. If you are already consumed, I want to empower you to start looking at the symbols and integers of your life. Take a deep look inside and do not decide just based on an experience or thought, but on evidence-based definitions. Be able to have courageous conversations with your loved ones. You want to be able to talk about whatever has happened in your life.

If something has happened that you are consumed by and you bring it into someone else's life and consume them with those things that are not truthful or factual, you are putting that person in a situation where his or her facts can never be true facts. You are robbing that person of his or her facts. When you are consumed by what you do not think you cannot control, you are also robbing yourself of the facts. You are robbing yourself of the truth. When you are consumed by what you believe you cannot control, you begin to camouflage, using tools and habits to cover up the truth. At some point, pain will override everything and every situation and will float like it has never floated before. That is why it is important to know the truth about the facts. That is the only way that you can control the integers or the symbols of your formula of facts.

CHAPTER 4

PIGS, BITCHES, AND SLAVES

"It is time to live your life by facing your truths and the facts of your life!"

HEY PIG! HEY BITCH! HEY SLAVE!

IF I WALKED up to you and called you a pig, what would you say? What if I called you a bitch? Would you try to do me bodily or psychological harm? Okay, maybe, but what if I called you a slave? How would that resonate with you? If I were a betting man, which I am not, I would bet that my calling you any of those names would get me in some big trouble with you! This chapter is going to be tough. I am letting you know early because I want you to have an open mind about what I am saying to you. Strap in, because I am going to provide valuable information that will better equip you to push through some of that dirt that we talked about in the first chapter.

At the beginning of the last chapter, I asked you to take an inventory of sorts of your own life. I followed those questions with a story of a young man who has been consumed by something that is out of his control for many years. I gave you a bird's eye view over the past 15 years of his life and illustrated the ways in which not honoring the facts of his life and his own truth have hampered his happiness, comfort, and ultimately, his identity.

I want you to think back to that young man's experience. Even though your story may not be as extreme as you perceive his story to be, you must know that there is at least one thing in your life that consumes you, but you have not yet mastered the way to control it. Really search your heart and mind for that truth for a minute. What is that one thing that you just have not been able to let go? As you embark on reading this chapter, I want you to invite that thing into your mental and emotional space. For the sake of your growth and your ability to deal with the truths and facts of your life, I am going to help you learn more about yourself so that you can move to a place of releasing that thing from your life.

The manifestation of being consumed by something, over which you believe you have no control, is what I like to call the Pig, Bitch, and Slave Syndrome (PBS). Now I know that is harsh language, but I really need you to follow me. I need you to fully understand this because your life depends on it. I want you to get this, so I am going to take some time and deal with each characteristic of PBS Syndrome.

We know that pigs wallow in mud and think that is where they belong. If you find that you are making a choice to stay in the position that you are currently in, even though it is not properly serving your life, you need to ask yourself if you are a pig. Really examine yourself here for a moment. If you like following the same routine, being in the same dead-end relationship or job, or just the same rut that you have been in for a while—and you have the option to move but you decide that you are going to stay there—you need to understand that you are acting like a pig.

A bitch, in this context, means that you know that you can do something better and that something greater is waiting for you if you just move! However, you continue to stay in the same mess. Now, the slave is like a Siamese twin to the bitch. The slave is like that elephant with a wet noodle around his neck, thinking that the noodle has all the power, when in fact, that does not make sense. How could something as big as an elephant be controlled by a tiny wet noodle? This is the overall concept of PBS Syndrome.

So, as you look at the truths and facts of your life, look at the ways in which you are operating as a pig, bitch, or a slave. Are you going to a job that you hate every single day because you believe that you must stay there, while knowing that your dream career is somewhere else? You may have convinced yourself that you have no other options or that you have painted yourself into a situation that you must now accept as final. Perhaps you are thinking that the choices that you have made up until this point in your life have led you to stay in that job anyway because you are not worthy of belonging anywhere else. If this resonates with you on a deep level, then you are most likely operating as a pig.

You may work in a career that affords you a very generous salary. You drive a beautiful luxury car and live in a beautiful home. You present very well with your style choices. You look good from the outside. However, behind all the glamor that you present to the world, you know that all five of your credit cards are maxed out. You know that if you were to be fired from your job today, you would not have enough money in your savings account to sustain your lifestyle for a month. You know that maintaining a good credit score and a sizable savings account is the smart thing to do and you have the financial means to do both, but you do not seem to care because you think you got it goin' on right now. You place more emphasis on spending than preparing for the future. You know better, but have no interest in doing better. You are operating as a bitch.

You may be in a situation where you feel you have no control. You may have convinced yourself that the situation is bigger than anything that you could even hope to overcome. Thus, you shrink who you are. You deny your own humanity. You bow down and give up. You are operating as a slave.

THE POWER OF IRRATIONAL THINKING

Now that I have shared detailed examples of PBS, I want you to know about the origins of this syndrome. PBS Syndrome has everything to do with the ways in which you think and the ways in which you process those thoughts. I want to introduce you to the concept of irrational thinking and how it negatively affects the truths and facts of your life. Irrational thinking occurs when you look at an event in your life and that event affects your feelings, which in turn affect your thoughts and your actions. Rational thinking occurs when you look at an event and the event affects your thoughts, which in turn affect your feelings and actions. I know that these may look very similar, but there is a stark difference between the two ways of thinking.

Most often people subscribe to irrational thinking when they feel wronged in a certain situation; allowing the precipitating event to create feelings about that event. Those feelings then put you in a position to create thoughts based solely on those feelings. Now, that you are fully involved in your feelings, you will find yourself acting in a way that is not at all beneficial to you. The prescribed way is to force yourself to think before you feel. You must make a dedicated decision to process things in a different way. I want to share a brief story about another client's experience with irrational thinking and how it affected the facts and truths of his life in a very negative way.

A gentleman was married with three children, ages six months, two years, and six years old. He and his wife were married for eight years. He was a laborer by trade, and by working overtime, he earned a six-figure salary. His wife was a stay-at-home mother to their three children and she took care of the maintenance of the home. His daily request was that he had cold beer and dinner waiting when he arrived home from work.

One day he came home and there was no beer, no dinner, and the house was in disarray, according to him. He became angry and an argument ensued. He explained to her that he worked hard to provide for her and the children, and the least she could do for him was to honor his simple daily request. After a few minutes of heated language, he slapped his wife. His wife had never been in a fight before in her life and was amazed that her husband would hit her. She made the decision to call the police. When the police arrived, they immediately noticed the handprint on the wife's face because of the slap, and the husband was arrested. Well, of course he made bail and had to go to court. The wife went all out and obtained a temporary restraining order on her husband. He was ordered to anger management, and that is how he became my client.

For weeks, he was angry because he had to attend anger management and take time off from work to fulfill his obligation to the court. He had mandatory overtime at his job, but he could not go because he had to work within the confines of my schedule for his court-ordered anger management sessions. His wife of eight years filed for divorce.

At about the midpoint of our sessions, it was like a lightbulb turned on and he could dig deeper into what really happened. When I asked him what the event was, he told me. When I asked him how he felt, he shared that he felt disappointed and disrespected. When I asked him how it made him think, he said that he thought that his wife did not care about him enough to honor his request, and that she did not understand how hard he worked for her and their children. When I asked him why he slapped her, he shared that he did it to get her attention. He did not intend to slap her, but he needed her to listen to him.

When he was younger, he saw his father strike his mother to get her attention. Essentially, he was acting in this way with permission from his previous experiences in his childhood home. I could see that he had finally figured it out, and I asked him what would he have done differently. He said that he had a niece that needed a job, and that he could have easily employed her to live with them to help his wife handle the management of the children and the home.

Once he figured it out, he realized that his wife had the equivalent of six jobs. Taking care of the individual and specific needs of each child was equal to three jobs. Taking care of herself and her husband was equal to two jobs. She also took care of the overall functioning of the house, which was equal to one very big job. So, he understood that she was working six jobs versus his one job. He had never thought about it in that way before. He only had feelings based on his personal perspective. The fact was that he was the bread winner. Another fact was he was the only one working. However, the truth was she was working very hard too, but she was just not earning a monetary income from her work.

The truth about it was that the wife had never experienced a fight with her husband, but she was always told by her father to never let a man raise his hand to her. Her father taught her that if it happened one time, it would happen again. The wife never gave her husband another opportunity to hit her.

Because my client did not examine the truths of the event, he lost his family. After working for 19 years at the same job, he was let go because his many court dates and anger management sessions led him to miss mandatory overtime and days at work. When his company had a round of layoffs, he was negatively impacted. He lost all the things that mattered to him because of one action. He had to use his 401(k) to pay alimony and child support payments. He lost because he did not deal with the truths of the facts. He now works at a convenience store and lives in an apartment. His life is vastly different than it was before he acted on his feelings one fateful day. He placed his feelings before his thoughts and the repercussions were devastating.

I WANT YOU TO LIVE

Living is about your existence. It is not just about whether your physical heart is beating. Living is also about the intangibles. These intangibles include your emotions and the ways in which you think about your life. Your physical heart may continue to pump blood and keep you alive physically according to God's plan, but what plan do you have to take control of your self-care and live a healthier life? What are you willing to do to maintain an emotionally healthy heart? What are you willing to do to have healthier relationships, healthier finances, and a healthier mindset?

What are you willing to do to maintain an emotionally healthy heart?

I want you to have healthier processes for your life, including beginning and ending relationships. There is a way to end relationships by telling the truth about why you no longer want to be in a relationship with that particular person. There is a process to achieving healthier relationships with the children that you have created, but do not provide any care for their upbringing. Part of that process is addressing the truths and the facts of why you have chosen to be an absent parent.

The truths about the facts are that you must really bear down and claw beyond the surface. Scratch until you get to the lower layers. This is a daily pursuit, and while it can be challenging, understand that it can also be rewarding and can provide you with the destiny in life that you desire or something that you cannot even imagine. I think a lot of times, we live beneath the potential of where we can go and what we can be because we are stuck. Our integers and symbols are stuck. We know that 1+1=2, and that is where we are determined to stay.

Remember that pig mentality? Know that you can switch those integers and symbols up completely and move beyond saying things like, "I'm too old to change." We also must stop saying, "I've been doing this so long that I'm not going to make any adjustments." We say things like, "There's nothing new under the sun," and we hold tight to those beliefs, but they are all lies.

We must subscribe to a new and improved method of thinking. Proverbs 23:7 (KJV) tells us that "As a man thinketh, so is he." This is not a religious book, but we subscribe to that principle. So, if you think lies, then you are a liar. That is a hard truth, but it is the truth. If you think health, you will be healthy because you will practice a lifestyle that will fully support that pursuit. If you are dealing with all the superficial things and things that are not truthful, you are just dealing with image stuff that will only get you from moment to moment or conversation to conversation. Stuff that gets you from check to check. You are not living that process of truths about the facts. You are lying to yourself and no one else. It is time to live your life by facing your truths and the facts of your life!

TIME TO REDEFINE YOU

I want you to redefine PBS and turn it into something positive. Instead of viewing yourself as a pig, bitch, or slave, I want you to view yourself as powerful, bold, and strong. So, what does that mean? When you begin to view yourself as powerful, you will create an opportunity to move out of that dead-end job. You will seek your heart's desire for your chosen career by any means necessary, and you will do what it takes to stop wallowing in the past like you used to do. Your truths and facts will change, and you will not only see yourself as powerful, you will become powerful. You will operate in that power and you will see the value in moving forward.

I want you to view yourself as powerful, bold, and strong.

When you are bold, you will take control of your finances, no matter your current financial situation. You will make it a point to direct money into your savings account with every direct deposit from your career. When you are bold, you will reprioritize and put less energy into putting on a show for others and more energy focusing on your internal happiness. You will pay off your debt, on time, and you will watch your credit score rise to heights that you never even imagined. You will be so bold with your finances that you will even forget that it is payday. You thought you had it goin' on before, but being bold will take you places beyond your imagination and set you up beautifully for retirement or being able to help others throughout your lifetime and beyond.

Remember that situation that threatened to hold you hostage forever? That circumstance that had you believing that you had to be a slave? When you are strong, you will say farewell to that situation. You will reclaim your control over the truths and facts of your life, and you will triumph.

Understand that being powerful, bold and strong will be a lifelong process. Sometimes you may even find yourself slipping back into that old Pig, Bitch, and Slave Syndrome, but you must continue to push through the dirt and remind yourself that you do not want to go back to that place. It will take work, but you are worth the effort.

CHAPTER 5

WHO AM I?

"I am the only one who can tell my story."

I GREW UP in North Carolina in a single-parent household. Although my mother was not single when I was born, I was raised by my single mother because my parents divorced when I was two years old. My dad did not participate in raising me physically or emotionally. I knew early on, as far back as kindergarten, that something was different about the dynamics of my family. I think that instinctively every child knows that when one parent is not there, that something is off. The truth about my family dynamic is that my parents divorced, and my dad was not a part of our lives.

Understanding and feeling that there was something different innately, caused me to have to think and process differently. I was wondering how this came to be. How am I here and it is just my mom? Where is the other person? I knew that it did not just happen in that way, even though I did not know about the birds and the bees at that point. I figured out early that there was a missing piece. Understanding and looking at things from that lens made me process differently, even to the point where doing homework, cleaning up, and communication was different, because a key figure who was supposed to be in my life was not there.

My mom tried to communicate like she was my mother and my father, which was confusing for me. She was doing the best she could, but it is not designed for one parent to take on the roles of both parents, no matter the circumstances. However the situation came to be, it is not designed for the family to be one-sided and to be managed from one perspective. Growing up, looking at things differently, and trying to figure out why this person is not there or why you never hear from this person, is difficult for a child. When you are thinking about your own family dynamics and comparing them to the families that you see on television, or your friends being dropped off at school by their fathers while you must ride the bus every day, you try to figure out why your life is so different.

The good thing about my mother is she did her best to explain everything to me and my sister, Crystal. She explained why turning off the lights before leaving the room or turning off the water if it was running was important, from a financial standpoint. If she had to work overtime, she explained why she had to work overtime. If she did not explain those things to us, it would have been an economic disaster for her. I learned a lot of different ways to processing life from a female single parent perspective. My mama was a radical. She often said that the Civil Rights Movement may have been a little too civil for her. Though she is now a born-again Christian, she was more radical when my sister and I were children. Even as a Christian, she has never subscribed to Christ's teaching of turning the other cheek. Her name is Dr. Brenda Rowdy, and her last name speaks for itself. She can be rowdy in a good way, but also rowdy in another way, if needed.

The past helps to shape your thinking, but for me, because I did not have one parent, I wanted to explain to my little friends why my dad was not taking me to Cub Scouts, or was not outside playing catch with me. I started to make excuses, and I learned early in life to camouflage.

A lot of times, as we grow into adults, we often must go back and dig into our childhoods to try to understand how we got to be the way that we are currently. I liked food growing up because food made me feel comfortable, which made me grow into an overweight person. I camouflaged my weight with clothes. I dressed up my body to hide. Because my family infrastructure was not there, I developed a way to camouflage how I communicated. I need you to understand that communication is just not in spoken language, it also incorporates how you dress, think, feel, listen, and evaluate. My foundation was off, and because of that, I could identify the facts of my life, but I was unable to identify how they became facts. That process was painful and unclear because I was missing parts of the story surrounding my father's absence from my life.

A lot of times, as we grow into adults, we often must go back and dig into our childhoods to try to understand how we got to be the way that we are currently.

I grew up in the church and was a child performing with a professional choir. I experienced things that most children do not get to experience at such a young age. I traveled with the choir and recorded songs as a professional with the choir. I sang with a variety of orchestras and celebrities. That became another camouflage to who I was. I got to do these things, which are facts, but it was not what I wanted to do. I really did not know what I wanted to do. I could not get to that because I could not deal with the origin and why my foundation was off. Why was I so concerned and consumed by what clothes and shoes I wore? What were people thinking about me? Were they laughing at me? Those questions came from my foundation. I did not have truth and because of that, I developed a way to camouflage what I did not know. I felt that it was not right, but I did not know how to talk about it, especially in my family dynamic.

I was in eleventh grade before I had any idea about what I wanted to do with my life. I was so consumed with being in the choir and being in church, that I really did not know there was a much bigger world. I am not saying that there is anything wrong with that. But, I did not have the regional, national and global cultural competencies to develop the values necessary to be the best at everything, not just a choir member or as a young man doing things in the church and the community. I did not have the competencies to be my best person holistically.

At this time, my mother started asking me about what I was going to do after high school. She always advocated attending college or enlisting in the military. I really wanted to go to the military, but the fact is physically I could not do it. The fact of the matter was that I had a bone deficiency in my knees that would keep me from passing the physical tests. I was in ROTC and was very successful. My idea was to go from ROTC to college, come out as a second lieutenant and make a career out of the military. One of the ROTC colonels at Hanes High School told me that I could complete ROTC because it would help me with leadership and discipline, but physically I was not military material. He also told me that I could do anything mentally.

That conversation changed my thinking and I knew that I had to change my game plan. That conversation led me to pursue the college route. College was not something that was really pushed in my community. I was always told to be a good person, treat people well, and do well in school, but I was never specifically told why it was important to do well in school. My mom did the best that she could with information, but she had me at nineteen when she was a freshman in college and she only completed one year. She completed her studies, but that was later in life.

There were five men who were instrumental in my life: Charles Jenkins, Larry Peebles, John P. Kee, Tony Pollard, and David Allen, who was a large part of my musical life. In the absence of my father, they taught me how to be a man. They taught me about how to work and how to think better. Even though they were there for me, I was troubled about why these outside people had to come and help me when my own father was not interested in helping me. That was a confusing piece for me. In that process, I could rebel and not subscribe to all their teachings because I had competing interests. I was always trying to figure out why the person who was supposed to be there was not there.

There were also limitations to the people who came into my life to help shape me. Because they had lives of their own, they had to take time out of their schedules to spend time with me. I was not their schedule. There is a difference. Fathers, when you create children, that is your schedule. You do not make time for the children, your children are your schedule. Understanding that influences your processes and thinking which influences your future. Your future becomes your legacy. What you do today inevitably becomes your history. How you think and how you process comes from your foundation.

Fathers ... you do not make time for the children, your children are your schedule.

I was blessed to have many men in my life to teach me and look out for my best interests. As no one is perfect, I learned both good and bad things from these men, but I was fortunate enough to have a wide range of good men to help shape my thinking. However, this came with a price because each one of them were different and I had to balance my thoughts between all of them, even when I had no idea what balance meant. They gave me a strong work ethic and helped me to understand the value of being a good man.

The process of getting to the truth about the facts stemmed from that. Even the times that I have done wrong in my life, it was never without feelings of guilt. If I did something wrong or told a lie to my mom, I would just tell the truth eventually because I just could not take it. These men helped to shape my moral compass. I realized that having a strong moral compass—that consciousness of wanting to do what's right—is when I constantly looked for truth, healing, and forward movement. I knew that I would not stay in that mental place forever, no matter my circumstances of having an absent father. I had the foundation of being around men and women to demonstrate that I had to move forward. I saw these men get off work and go to work. That is what I saw, which taught me to leave school in the afternoons and go to work.

I want to share this story with you. In the ninth grade, I was retained. I was not retained because I could not do the work, I was just more invested in singing and being in the professional choir because it helped my image and popularity. We would appear on television occasionally and I just wanted to hang out and travel. If there was a performance going on, I would try to be there, which resulted in me not doing my homework. I would then try to convince the teachers that I had a busy professional schedule, not realizing that was not what I was supposed to be doing.

I think a lot of that is due to my foundation. I was confused about what I should have been doing because I did not have the information. I created processes in my mind that led me to believe that if I could explain things well, people would buy into what I was selling, but that was not the truth. I was trying to justify not doing my homework because I was using singing and church as excuses. This justification of doing what I thought was the right thing, instead of the right thing *academically*, created this situation of being retained.

This created a new situation because my sister Crystal was only one year behind me. I was semi-popular in school, so how was I going to hide the fact that I had been retained? Well, I learned to cover. I was so clever that I arrived to school early, went to my home room teacher and told her my situation. I told her that I knew I had to check in, but if I checked in when the other students were present, everybody was going to know that I was still in the ninth grade. I asked her if I could just come by and wave my hand and then go on to my first period class and just sit there until class started. She probably should not have, but she allowed me to do that to protect me. So, I learned how to cover up because I did not like the truth. The fact of the matter was that I was retained, and I just should have dealt with that.

Now, there was one teacher who I could not fool. The librarian at Hanes High School in Winston Salem, North Carolina, was not to be fooled by my cover. She pulled me over in a room in the library, and jacked me up and said, “I heard that your big ass got retained!” She said, “You singing on the choir and these people are looking up to you, but you done got your big ass retained, so what you gonna do about it?” When she said that to me, I began to cry because my cover was blown. I never even told my mama that I was retained. I could hide it so well.

The librarian advised me to go to alternative school in the evening to catch up and get moved up to the tenth grade. She told me where to go and when to be there. She even set it all up for me. And guess what? The alternative school was en route to church. In the evenings, I would leave the apartment and walk to church to clean up and then attend the alternative school. I liked having the attention of the bishop and people knowing that I was a good kid.

I became consumed by the accolades and attention that I received from the people at church, but it kept me from what I was supposed to do. What I was really looking for was accolades and attention from my father. That was the truth about the facts. So, I enrolled in this alternative school, completed the work, and made all A's. Before Thanksgiving, I had already caught up on a year's worth of work to advance to the tenth grade. Going into the second semester, I would be in the tenth grade. I kept that a secret for years! Only my sister knew. God bless her heart because she was my confidante!

My mama always taught us to stick close to each other and Crystal did not let me down. I had to deal with the truths of that whole ordeal. I was looking for validation and accolades, and I did not get them from school, I got them from church. I should have done what I was supposed to be doing to get what I needed from every area. I am not blaming this on my parents' divorce, but it did have an impact on me because my father did not help to influence and shape me.

My father's absence impacted my processes and led to me not being able to express my real feelings. I became great at being able to sell and justify what I needed, but I needed to express that I needed love and that I was not happy about some things. I thought that if I masked my needs, I would be perceived in a certain way that was beneficial to me. I always worked and had money to buy the stuff for myself that my mother could not afford. At times, I would help my mother with a bill or two or give her gas money as a kid, before I could even drive.

The truth of the matter is that all I wanted was validation, information, and education. I wanted validation from an intangible perspective. I wanted to know how to grow up, how to be a man, how to be a lover, provider, and friend. I believe this is one of the problems that we have in our society. We become great at not dealing with the truths about the facts. We identify the facts, but we do a horrible job of dealing with the truths. We are not transparent about those truths and we do not confess those truths.

To this day, my daily process is making sure that I am transparent with myself first.

In 1993, I studied abroad at the American University in Cairo, Egypt, as part of my studies at the University of Hawaii, Manoa. I was supposed to study abroad for a year, but due to the political conditions in Cairo at that time, I returned to Hawaii early.

When I returned to the University of Hawaii, I did not have housing. I lived with a family for a few weeks, but that did not work out because they wanted me to pay rent and I had no money. I checked into the YMCA for one night. I remember I walked out of the YMCA and sat on the brick wall facing the mall. It was raining that day and I remember crying. I was reflecting on the good things that I had done since attending the University and my general popularity there, but I had no place to go but the YMCA. I did not know how to tell anyone. This went back to my foundation of hiding the truth.

As I sat there, a friend of mine who played basketball for Hawaii Pacific University and originally told me not to live with the family that I stayed with anyway, happened to ride by in his car. He asked me what was going on. I explained my situation to him because I knew I only had money for one night at the YMCA and I had no place to go. After that night, I was literally going to be on the streets. He invited me to hang out with him and his friends. I did not ask him what that meant; I was just so grateful that someone said, "Come with me." We went to the apartment and I literally had to sleep on a sofa on a porch. My duffle bag was my pillow and my towels were my blanket. He had several roommates, so it was basically just a place to lay my head after staying on campus all day.

During the time that I was living on that porch, I experienced a miracle. I must talk about this because I remember going to the pay phone outside of Sinclair Library to call my godbrother, Hiawatha Hemphill. He was getting his Master of Divinity at Lynchburg University in Virginia. I wanted to let him know that I was okay. I could not let my mom know the situation because there was nothing that she could do, and it would have worried her to death. Well, it cost me about $3.75 to make a long-distance call from the pay phone. When I hung up with my godbrother, the phone gave me back five dollars in quarters. That five dollars allowed me to go to Star Market, and I would buy a sub sandwich or a large piece of fish to cook. Whatever I purchased, I would cut it up into three pieces so that I could have breakfast, lunch, and dinner. The miraculous thing that happened is that every day that semester, I would call my godbrother and the phone would give me between five to seven dollars in change every day.

Now, I had a lot of friends, but it seemed like I could not find a friend on the island. I tried to find them, but I just could not find them. It was a wilderness experience for me of how to get to the truths of things. This phone booth allowed me to eat and wash my clothes. I would save a quarter a day so that by the end of the week, I could wash my clothes. I had to take a golf class to take a shower at school. I remember one of the janitors approached me and asked if I was okay. She noticed that I had been hanging my clothes and letting them steam while I showered. She told me to turn on all the showers to get more steam to get them clean. I was the only one using the showers anyway. I had to learn how to be homeless. I had to learn how to live in survival mode because I did not have all the things that everybody else had. I went from being at home and studying in Cairo, being in student government and doing good things, to being invisible among everybody. People knew me, but they could not see me because I did not tell the truth. They could see parts of me, but they could not see the truth, and as a result, they could not help me.

The last week of the semester, I received a letter from financial aid delivered to the place where I was sleeping on the porch. The letter informed me that all the red tape had been cleared and I had a refund check. I also received a letter from the housing office that informed me that I had a place to stay. In a day, my life changed. The first thing that I did was to go to financial aid to get my check, and I took it to the bank to cash it. I went back to that same phone booth that I had used all semester and it had an out of order sign on it. I become emotional every time I talk about it because being homeless taught me how to trust God. You can hear your mama talk about miracles and faith all you want, but until you experience a miracle for yourself, you really do not understand.

Years later, after getting married, buying a house, and moving to Florida, I became sick in 1997. I was roughly 340lbs, working long hours for an insurance company, and making good money. I was dressing in custom-made suits and even started a custom tailoring business. I was really busy, but I got sick to the point that I could not work. I was totally blind for four months. So, here I was again going through another crisis, but the crisis was now physiological. I had never dealt with the truths of my weight issues and that weight had been housing diabetes, heart disease, and other ailments. Because I could not work, I decided to return to school at the University of Hawaii. Our house rented out very quickly and our car sold quickly as well. Everything was falling into place, although my health was still bad.

We moved back to Hawaii and I started pursuing my Master's degree. My very first day back in Hawaii I realized that my blood pressure was stable, and I needed something to do. The first job I found was a recruiting job in the School of Social Work. Although I planned to get my degree in Sociology and really knew very little about social work, I interviewed and was hired. Mari Ono gave me a PowerPoint® presentation and told me to learn it and everything else that I could learn about social work. As I started reading and studying the material, I realized the connections between the two fields. I decided to pursue social work because I knew that I would be good at it.

That same week, I was on campus and I ran into a faculty member named Randy Chamblis who asked me where I had been because he had not seen me in a long time. As I began to tell him my homeless experience that I wore as a badge of honor, he said the following to me, "I don't ever want to hear that bullshit you're telling me because nobody knew that you were homeless. You didn't say a word. I had a place for you to stay. You chose to be in that space because you didn't tell the truth. You hid that from us. So, we can have a different conversation, but we aren't having this conversation." I really heard what he said. That is the truth about the facts. All I had to do was tell the truth about my situation, but because I learned how to camouflage at a young age, I did not know how to express my pains, anxieties, and challenges that I was going through.

To the readers of this book, you know that you are a good person, but you have these little vices and little things that you do, and you keep doing them. It's time to examine the truths of your past. It is about you! For me, it was not about my dad not being there. Some of the decisions I made were simply because I chose to do it as it was what I wanted. The important thing about parenting is identifying what you want instead of leaving it up to the child to figure out what they want, because when a child is left up to his own "infinite wisdom," that child will make mistakes and learn how to lie and camouflage. That child may even become successful at camouflaging, but there will be pieces in his or her life that will not work because of that.

Before you act, understand what your thinking is, and allow your thinking to drive your feelings and your feelings to dictate your actions.

As I talk about my past, I want you think about whatever your specific situation may be. Before you act, understand what your thinking is, and allow your thinking to drive your feelings and your feelings to dictate your actions. I am still a work in progress and I always will be. I am the only one who can tell my story. I encourage you to tell your own story, but you must tell the truth about your facts. If you are homeless, say that you are homeless. If you are broke, say that you are broke. If you are lonely, say that you are lonely. If you are in a situation that you do not want to be in, say that you do not like it, but dig down deep and tell the truth about why. That is where the story is. The truth about those things is where the healing is.

CHAPTER 6

FINDING YOUR TRUTH IN YOUR CURRENT STATE

"Start with yourself. Start naked. Start with zero."

WHEN YOU LOOK at the past, it is an indicator of where your future is headed. Until you decide to deal with the truth about your facts, your future is dim, cloudy, complex, and unclear. You may look up one day and wonder what you are going to do with your life. You may be in your late thirties and forties and you have lived a certain way for many years. You are starting to realize that the way you have always lived your life is no longer working for you, and you know that you need to make some changes to be happy and whole. You may even be consumed by what you think you cannot control because you have not discovered the truths about your facts or even put forth any energy to think about those truths. You may be in a relationship that you do not want to be in or maybe you have worked a job too long and did not prepare yourself with the adequate education to change careers. You see yourself as too old to do anything different and you fear failure.

Maybe you created bad debt that you are paying for, but you cannot pay enough down to escape. You have not saved an adequate amount of money to take care of your finances should some crises arise. Your income may be decent, but you know that you are worth more and you deserve more. You may notice that you have bad relationships and that your health is challenged. I know that all of this may sound bad, but it is as bad as it may seem. The examples that I shared are the types of things that cause all of us to make changes. At this stage of life, you begin to think more seriously about your health, education, socioeconomic status, where you live, and what you will look like in the future.

The older you become, the less time you have. When you are twenty-five years old, you may believe that you have fifty years to go, but when you are forty-five years old, you are primarily convinced that you no longer have fifty years to gain control of your life. When you are fifty, you know that you have reached middle age and your time to get things right is starting to become limited. Those numbers keep shrinking and you start to have anxiety about your current state. You try to figure out what you are going to do, and you start to panic. You start trying different things and that can create confusion and another set of false truths. You begin to choose your mate because you need a better today and a better future, when the truth of the matter is that you need to reengineer your life from ground zero. You need to give up the image, give up the look and the false belief that you must have a certain car, handbag, pair of shoes, or a huge home to be happy. You must find the strength within to dig beyond the surface level so that you can reengineer your life and hit the reset button. Allow yourself the space and opportunity to hit reset, knowing that this time you have your past and your history as a guide. You no longer must make the same mistakes that you did before. Remember, you do not have to compromise your principles, time, or your sanity to find happiness.

You need to give up the image, give up the look and the false belief that you must have a certain car, handbag, pair of shoes, or a huge home to be happy.

At this point, you have the truths about your facts. It is now time to start dealing with those truths and dig down into who you are. Learn your character as you dig past what people see and admire about you and into the stuff about you that other people do not know. Start with yourself. Start naked. Start with zero. Stop thinking and worrying about what people think. If someone loves and cares about you, they should love you regardless of your socioeconomic status.

If you feel like you must go out and hang with a certain crowd, and drink certain types of drinks to be successful, to be acknowledged, or to be a part of something, look at your history. You may find that you are looking for validation from a parent or a loved one, but it is manifesting in a way that has you looking for validation through a drink, promiscuity, gambling, or having a big social life. You are spending money and social capital that you do not have. You are spending health capital that you do not have. You are spending spiritual capital that you do not have. As your years get shorter, you realize that all those capitals are empty, because you spent them all on nothing meaningful.

Men, don't date because of the look of a potential partner. Do not focus on the curves, the hips, the breasts, and the sexual experience. Sure, those aspects are important, but do not let sex, money, and appearances be your guide to happiness, and do not let sex, money, and appearances be your truths. Although they are a part of your truth, do not let those details be the determining factors of choosing a mate. All that I have mentioned will change and run out. You may find yourself creating families that you abandon. Children are born that you may make time for, but know that you do not make time to be involved in the lives of your children; children are your time. If you are not prepared to behave accordingly, you have some more digging to do.

Women, do not date because of his six pack. As I shared with the men, there is nothing wrong with appreciating a handsome man with an attractive physique, but at some point in time, that six pack will go away. What will you be left with when that time comes? Is there a brain left? Is there a heart left? Is this someone who will massage, manage, and sustain your emotions? Is it someone who will take care of you holistically? Will you be involved with someone who is committed to you daily? If you change today or suffer an illness today, will he change for the worse or will he change with you? Will he become fluid like water?

With truth, you become fluid like water and you can get through and you can go over, under, lift, and penetrate anything with it. You can even penetrate the courageous conversations, difficult situations like divorce, and even special circumstances, but you must always start with truth. The truth is something that must be consistent and repetitive. If you are not prepared to date based on substance instead of aesthetics, you also have more digging to do.

Hit that reset button on your life right now. Acknowledge and honor the truths about your facts. You have no reason to be embarrassed about anything that you have experienced or overcame. You cannot change the past, but you can live a full life now, while you are diligently preparing for your future.

CHAPTER 7

FINDING YOUR TRUTH IN YOUR FUTURE STATE

"Make time to do anything else, but be time for your family."

AS YOU LOOK toward your future, you must know what your past has been. You must see yourself beyond your circumstances. Even when you are consumed by what you think you cannot control, one way to see light is to start to imagine your desired self. If you can see your desired self in your imagination, you can get to it. It is going to take truth. It is going to take you dealing with all the things in your life that have prevented you from getting to where you think you should be or where you want to be.

Stop giving yourself an excuse to say you cannot do something. You did not have a father, so you cannot be a good father to your own children. You had torn relationships, so you cannot trust anymore. You have always had to scrape and live from paycheck to paycheck, and that is why you are struggling. You do not study well, and that is why you did not pursue the career as a doctor that you always wanted. Stop giving yourself those excuses not to try. Throw everything against the wall and if it does not stick, pick it up and throw it against the wall again. Listen, there is something so special about you. You are the only person like you in this big and beautiful world.

Throw everything against the wall and if it does not stick, pick it up and throw it against the wall again.

Perhaps you do not realize the power that you have. Remember in chapter four, I encouraged you to be powerful, bold, and strong. Here is your chance to walk in that with your shoulders pushed back and your head held high. You had enough courage to dig below the surface of your dirt to find your truth. That is something to celebrate. You have developed a secret sauce that only you could create because the ingredients contain your facts and your truths. That secret sauce is what you have used to get you through those tough areas in your life. You are facing your fears. When you first threw your ideas and dreams against the wall and they did not stick, I bet you forgot to put your special sauce on it. Try it again and again, and add more sauce if you must, but do it until those ideas and dreams stick.

What goals have you set? When you set a goal, don't set one that you cannot give away. Goals that you keep to yourself make you selfish. If you cannot give it away, it is not a goal; it is a self-serving act. If your goal is to buy a car, start thinking about how you can pay it forward. After you have paid off that car, you can give it to your child or someone in your family that needs a car and does not have the financial means to pay for one. Have a mission with your goal to benefit something or someone else. If you are pursuing a degree or a job, ask yourself why. When I pursued my MSW, it was not just so that I could have a career, but it was also something that I was called to do. I was called to help people. While I do benefit, my ultimate goal is to give back. I do not think there is a goal you can have without giving it away.

Parents are often consumed with giving their children the best car and the latest and greatest styles. However, the children do not get the information about what it took for you to get those things for them, so they grow up thinking that getting everything that they want should be automatic. They pick friends that also think in the same manner. What happens is that they develop a way of thinking that does not consider other people.

I think that is one of the things that is plaguing our society now. We lack other-people thinking, whereas years ago, it was nothing to knock on your neighbor's door to ask for a cup of sugar. Today, not many people are going to their neighbors asking for some sugar or two eggs or loaf of bread, because they do not want people to know that they do not have those necessities. We have lost that honesty and those truths. When we lose truths, we lose the abilities to share and be transparent. We lose the ability to love and to receive love when we do not tell the truth.

When a woman is trying to build a relationship with a man, she puts her best self forward in all aspects. Don't change once you are securely in that relationship. In my world of social work, I often hear clients say things like, "This is how he or she started out, but it is different now." It is like the couple is realizing that they must make time for each other. We know we all must work, but when you are working you must have the mindset that you are working for your family. You are working to make sure that the bills are paid on time. You are working to make sure that you can treat your family to nice things and provide an education. You are working to provide whatever is needed. You are doing it in time, for time to be spent with your family.

If you believe that you must make time, that person or your family is an afterthought. Anytime that someone is an afterthought, you will not honor them. If you bought flowers in year one, what has happened in year three? If you were calling every day in the beginning, what is different now? You must be even more intentional about maintaining that relationship. If you cannot keep up and do better from where you began, you should not be in a relationship. You will only have a *making tim*e type of mentality. Make time for your work. Make time to work out. Make time to go shopping. Make time to do anything else, but be time for your family. When we look at how God treats us, we will realize that we are his time. We are his singular focus. He is all in with us. When we are sick, when we are hurting, and when we are not paying him any attention; when things are good or bad, in crisis or not, we are his time regardless of time. That should be our model. Be time for your family. Even if you are not there physically, you cannot use that as an excuse. This allows you to be creative. Send flowers to represent your love and appreciation if you cannot be there. Call ahead to a favorite restaurant and pay for dinner for your family. While they are enjoying their food, call them on FaceTime® or another video chat app and have dinner with them virtually. Make sure to show love all the time.

CHAPTER 8

THE SPIRIT OF HEALING

"That space between truth and facts is called life."

WHEN WE TALK about the spirit of healing, we must first identify what needs to be healed and why. It must be a mission. Whether the pain manifests as physical, emotional, or mental pain, you must determine in your mind that you want to be healed. Sometimes there is no cure, answer, alternative treatment, or antidote to heal some physical and mental pains; however, there is something about the spirit that can heal us emotionally, if that is your desire and hope.

I want to share a story about how the spirit of healing helped me to face my own truths and facts about my life. I've known a man that I greatly admired since I was nine years old. I knew him from my experiences of being in a professional choir, so I really only knew him from a distance. From that distance, he was an icon and someone that I aspired to be like in terms of talent. I knew his personality from a 30,000-foot view as a child, never imagining that I would come to know him on another level as an adult.

After many years of knowing him, the view from which I knew him gradually decreased from 30,000 feet to 10,000 feet. After more time, 10,000 feet became 5,000 feet, and eventually 5,000 feet became 1,000 feet. We stayed at 1,000 feet because we never had that real close relationship that I would have enjoyed. I think a lot of it was because he did not have a relationship with his father. This was a man who visibly knew how to communicate with a crowd, but was challenged on a more personal level. As I reflect now, I realize that I viewed this man as a mentor because that is something that I needed; however, he never actually agreed to mentor me.

He was more of a friend from an older generation. Still, that expectation remained, if only viewed from the lens through which I wanted my needs to be met. Had he agreed to be my mentor, I do not think that he would have been fully equipped to provide that level of mentoring for me, but I still looked at him as someone from whom I wanted guidance. I never took it personally and I never judged him, because after looking at him from a 1,000-foot view, I knew that I had to look at him from a different perspective. I looked at myself, too, because I understood what he was going through because he didn't know his father or his mother. I understood the dynamics of not having a father. Though older and wiser than I in a variety of areas, I may have had more insight into how to communicate on a personal level than he did.

I admired his business acumen, and I wanted to be included in his business deals and business meetings because I knew that I had the knowledge to really push the business further. While others were invited to be a part of this inner circle, I was not. I can only surmise that because I was significantly younger, he was unsure of the value that I could add to his business ventures. I had a difficult time trying to understand why I was being underestimated and shutout, and eventually abandoned the desire to be a part of his professional life in that capacity. I kept those thoughts and feelings to myself. It created a level of pain within me, and I didn't know how to effectively communicate with him because I was unsure about how to approach the situation. Maybe all that was necessary was for me to make him aware that he was treating me differently than I, or even he, may have anticipated. Instead, I left it alone.

He was a very successful man and I valued his opinions, but there were a lot of times when he expressed his views on my educational background and chosen career from a judgmental position. He referred to my work as a community activist as poverty work, and referred to me as a poverty professional. While he may not have meant any harm, it created a space between truth and facts for me. The fact was that I was not being treated the way I felt I should be treated, but the truth was I had no idea why.

There were many times that I wanted to help him in other ways in his life. I knew of certain ways that I could be of help to him, but I stopped extending myself to him because it was never embraced. From my perspective, there did not appear to be any value in what I could offer to him. I did not want to pursue it because, as I shared in chapter five, I wanted to be validated. My mission was to find those areas that validated me, and for me, that was my work.

There is a common thread between men and women who grow up without their fathers. They are either overachievers or underachievers, because they are looking for validation. When you do not receive that validation, you will either fight for it or you will give up on it. Sometimes you may find that you are doing both, by overachieving on certain things for a period and underachieving on other things for a certain period.

I always respected him, and I always included him on anything that I was doing, but I wondered in the back of my mind why I could not be included on the things that he was doing. The people around him were included, whether it was a business idea or concept he was working on, and he would invite someone who may not have even had the skill set, network connections, or knowledge base to do what he needed done. At least that is what I thought and felt, although they could have been equipped to execute his plans correctly.

The truth of the matter is that I should have dealt with those thoughts and feelings from the beginning, but I did not know how to deal with it because my foundation did not include that ingredient and neither did his. We were men lacking a certain foundational ingredient and it took a crisis to bring healing. That crisis came when he became ill, and at that point, I had to decide what to do. It was my calling, not my chore, to be present with him during his illness. I soon discovered that while his family loved him and cared for him, I had the best skill set. I had to make the decision to either go all-in with someone who called me a poverty professional and who did not include me in on things. During the time of his illness, I had to decide to give full care or give some care. As a caregiver, you can choose to do one or the other.

One day when we were on the way to the hospital, he asked me if I was going to stick with him through his illness. During that ride, he also told me that he wanted to write a book. I thought it would be good for his mental health. He asked me and other family members to write an excerpt in his book. I wrote about the spirit of healing. When he presented my excerpt to his publisher, the publisher did not want to include it because he thought it was a separate book. It did not flow with the rest of the book that he was writing, but he encouraged me to write a book. *The Truth About the Facts*, the book that you are now reading, is inspired by him because I got to see, up close and personal, how he was trapped between truth and facts on so many levels. While he was a great businessman and a great family provider, he too, was trapped between truth and facts.

I visited Hawaii to conduct a training. I remember that when I arrived back to my hotel room, it was still daylight. After looking out over the Pacific Ocean, I went inside, got down on my knees, and asked God to heal me. I remembered someone shared with me about fire in Hawaii. The person told me that there were three types of fire. A yellow heat can burn rubber, blue heat is enough to burn steel, and white heat is pure heat. I asked God to give me white heat, so that I could give all and not be consumed by what I thought I could not control, which was lack of communication, not knowing, and my history.

I asked God to give me a spirit of healing, not just for the person whom I admired as a mentor, but for me to give to other people. I prayed for God to give me white heat for my own father, so that I could get past him being abusive to my mom. I needed that white heat so that I could get past him kicking my mom in the stomach while she was carrying me, in an effort to abort me. I had to, and I continue to ask God for white heat to give me pure joy and love. The kind of joy and love that could make my spirit pure. While I am not perfect, I do want to be clean. Now I know that is metaphoric, but it is true. As I talk about the spirit of healing, my pursuit is to be clean, but not perfect.

My godfather and great friend, D.J. Rogers wrote a song that said, "I just want to be clean inside." I may not be perfect on the outside, in fact I never will be, but I must get to clean. This is a daily pursuit. I encourage you to get to clean. Find clean between truth and facts. The only way to do that is to identify the truths about the facts. You must get in that space and be truthful and transparent with yourself through all the pains, through the joys, through whatever it is, and fight in that space! Do not lie about your space, instead share and communicate about your space. Believe in your space because it is not all bad. You will never fully get out of that space. That space between the truth and the facts is called life.

Whether you were molested as a child, abused as an adult, lied to, or misunderstood, find your freedom in the spirit of healing. That space is between truth and facts. That is where the spirit of healing is. If you do not deal with the truth, however, the spirit of healing will not show up. You will always have that emptiness and that void. Your story may not be like mine, but we all have some issues and some pain.

As I close this book, I hope that you have gained some insight about the truths and the facts of your life. I hope that you have allowed yourself to be vulnerable and open to the things that I have shared. I want you to dream, pursue your passions, and thrive. I want you to have grace for yourself as you seek out your truths and facts. I want you to take the spirit of healing with you always. When you start to drift back into old patterns, I hope that you will pick up this book and read it again. You never know what you will find the second or third time around. Some new things may resonate with you and you may be awakened to new possibilities. Walk in your freedom and bask in the knowledge that every day you are learning to love yourself more and more.

ABOUT THE AUTHOR

Dr. Leven "Chuck" Wilson II, MSW, is the CEO and President of CPAG Inc., a healthcare business solutions firm providing case management, organizational development, and process transformation consulting utilizing Lean Six Sigma methodologies. As an entrepreneur, he has implemented strategies to address revenue cycle management needs targeting healthcare businesses. With over 15 years of service and experience in the healthcare industry, Dr. Wilson's professional expertise includes gerontology, consulting in crisis management, and community development on a micro-macro-mezzo level. He serves on multiple boards and consults on business strategies, providing a targeted approach to corporate operations. His processes have been instrumental to many projects becoming prototypes for community initiatives.

Dr. Wilson actively serves as the senior executive advisor of The Renew Group, which is a (501c3) non-profit operation dedicated to changing lives and communities on a national level. He received recognition as Social Worker of the Year in 2013 citing his professional, social, and personal impact on the communities he serves. Dr. Wilson travels to Haiti annually to assist in providing tents, medicine and tools used for daily living. Dr. Wilson has partnered with the Conservation Fund of North Carolina and the Kenan Institute at the University of North Carolina Chapel Hill to develop an Agriculture Center in a tier one county in northern North Carolina.

Dr. Wilson received his Bachelor of Arts in Sociology and a Masters of Social Work degree from the University of Hawaii at Manoa. Mr. Wilson has postgraduate work at Oxford Graduate School. Dr.

Wilson received a Doctorate of Humane Letters from Virginia University of Lynchburg. He is a former Faculty Member and Principal Investigator at the School of Social Work at the University of Hawaii at Manoa where he developed and deployed a Multicultural Communications Series. He received recognition from the Senate and House Representative in Hawaii for his service to the underserved in the community.

Some of his major partnerships to address health, economic, social justice, and environmental disparities include healthcare providers, communities, municipalities, universities, National Football League, and ecumenical institutions nationally. He is also actively engaged in community development consulting initiatives with Moffitt Cancer Center, Town of Garysburg, Pasco-Hernando State College, Eckerd Foundation, Veterans Affairs Administration, Office of Public Guardian, Department of Public Safety, Conservation Fund of North Carolina, Department of Health and Human Services, Yale University School Development Program, Duskin AINOWA Foundation based in Japan, University of Hawaii at Manoa, and the Carolina Panthers.

For speaking engagements, conferences, book signings, and to add your location to the national book tour, contact:

Robin Wise at 813.997.9893
E-mail: rwise@renewgroup.org

Other Authors by

Fallen Chains
Samantha Campbell
ISBN ~ 978-0997992366

The Comback
Darrin Williams
ISBN ~ 978-0997992328

Early Morning Visitor
Rolinda Butler
ISBN ~ 978-0997992304

The Love Between
Tiffany Hayes
ISBN ~ 978-0997992342

Devastated But Not Destroyed
Jessica Jones
ISBN ~ 978-0692342015

Daily Dose of Direction for Women in Business
Melanie Bonita
ISBN ~ 978-0998831305